Write about Me

Elsie S. Wilmerding

EDUCATORS PUBLISHING SERVICE
Cambridge and Toronto

Acknowledgments

I would like to acknowledge Nancy M. Hall for

continually giving me encouragement.

Acquisitions/ Development: Sethany Rancier
Editor: Jean O'Halloran
Managing Editor: Sheila Neylon
Typesetting: Rebecca Royen

ISBN 0-8388-2622-9
978-0-8388-2622-5

5 6 7 8 PPG 10 09 08

For the Teacher

In *Write about Me*, young writers are asked to think about themselves and to examine their own environment because this is what they know best.

Write about Me is an introduction to the process of writing that evolved from working and writing with elementary school children. Sometimes young writers have difficulty generating or organizing ideas in written form. This task is often alleviated when the child is first asked to draw a picture of an idea as a prewriting activity. Visualizing is one strategy to help prepare for writing.

During the process of visualizing, most children are able to invent and illustrate a central topic, and with encouragement, are capable of adding details to a picture for enrichment. Verbalizing and translating ideas from pictures into sentences are helpful to the whole writing process.

Organizing and sequencing thoughts is an ongoing task. Drawing, listing, and mapping are strategies that contribute to the brainstorming process. This workbook is a straightforward presentation of suggestions to help the writer generate and organize beginning seeds of thoughts.

Please note that on the final page of this book you will find a list of words that might be difficult for your students to read. Some are sight words and some are multisyllabic words. Try introducing two or three words at a time, so students will be familiar with the words by the time they meet them in the workbook.

Contents

Introduction

You are becoming a writer. A good way to begin writing is to think about yourself and your own world. To do this, you must always *look* and *listen* carefully to everything around you. Looking and listening will help your writing. When you write about yourself and your world, you will be able to use the details that you see, hear, and even smell. For example, when you see a garden, you see pink or red or white flowers. Think about the difference between hearing a scream or a whisper. You may wake up and smell bacon one day or cinnamon toast the next. Adding these details to your writing makes it real and believable.

Sometimes the process of thinking and putting ideas into written words may seem difficult, but with practice it gets easier. Drawing pictures, making lists, and creating maps will help you think of what you want to say. In this book, you will have a chance to try these things. You will see how ideas can turn into pictures and then into stories. Your writing might be a simple list, a note, or a story. Writing will help you say what is inside your head, and it will show your reader what you see and hear in your world. As you begin to write, many writing ideas will pop into your mind. Don't let them go away! Turn to page 57 at the end of your book and write the ideas that you may want to use later. It is a good place to store your thoughts.

Have fun!

All about Me

My name is _____ .

I am _____ years old.

I go to _____ School.

I am in grade _____ .

Here is a picture of me:

1

My eyes are _____ .

My skin is _____ .

My hair is _____ .

My friend _____ measured me.

I am _____ tall.

I am as tall as _____ .

I am shorter than _____ .

I am heavier than a _____ .

I write with my _____ hand.

(right or left)

Here is an old photograph of me taken when I was younger:

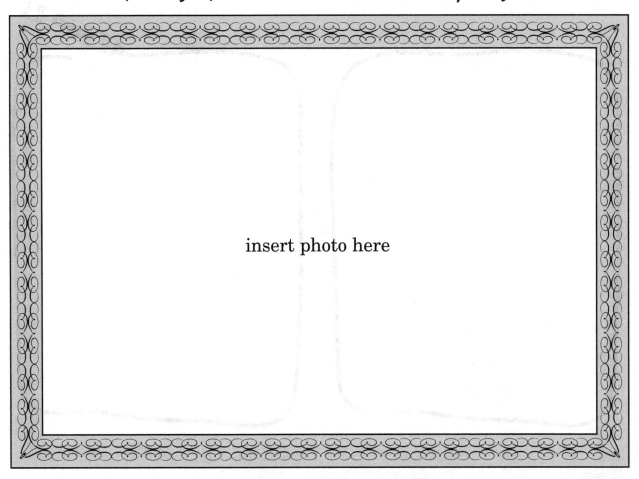

I am the same person, but I have changed since that photograph. These are some of the ways that I have changed:

_____
- -
_____
- -
_____
- -
_____
- -
_____
- -
_____

Here are pictures of two things that are too small for me now:

✎ Write about the pictures above.

Fill in the blanks with the correct numbers:

I have _____ sister(s).

I have _____ brother(s).

I have _____ pet(s).

Here is a picture of the people and pets who live with me:

These are the names of the people and pets who live with me:

My Neighborhood

My town or city is called _____ .

The name of my street is _____ .

What do you live near? Do you have **neighbors**? Your home and the things near your home make up your neighborhood. For example, Matt lives near a playground and a bank, but Emma lives near a barnyard filled with chickens.

Here are some things you may see in your neighborhood:

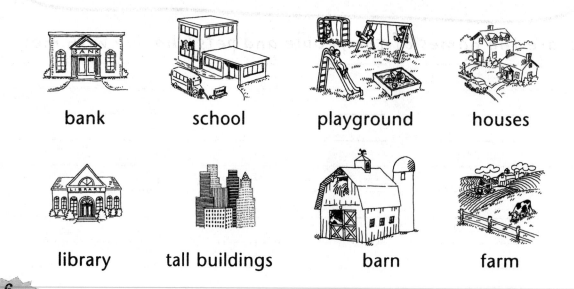

bank   school   playground   houses

library   tall buildings   barn   farm

Draw a picture of your neighborhood. Include your home and things near your home.

These are some things in my neighborhood:

_____   _____

-------------------------------   -------------------------------

_____   _____

_____   _____

-------------------------------   -------------------------------

_____   _____

_____   _____

-------------------------------   -------------------------------

_____   _____

My Day

How do you spend your day? Use the boxes to draw about your day.

Think about what you do in the morning, afternoon, and night.

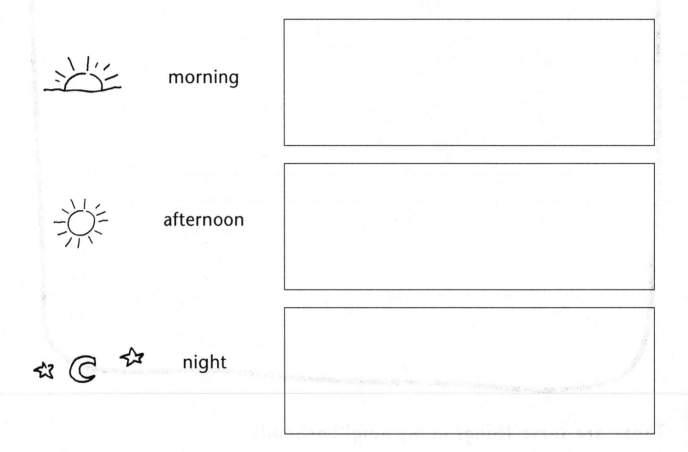

morning

afternoon

night

Now circle the box that shows your favorite time of the day.

This is my favorite time of day because _____

_____

_____ .

My Favorites

My favorite color is _____ .

Here is something I like that is my favorite color:

My favorite toy or game is _____.

I like it because _____.

Here is a picture of it:

My favorite book or story is _____.

Here is a picture of one of my favorite parts in the story:

✏️ Write about your picture.

_____

- -

_____

_____

- -

_____

_____

- -

_____

Here is a picture of one of my favorite parts in a movie:

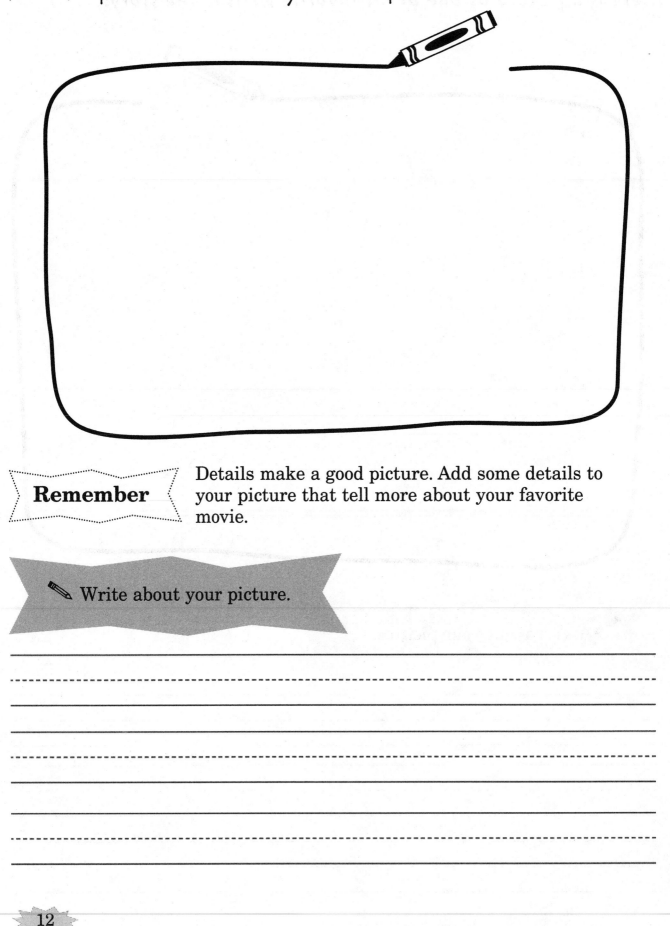

Details make a good picture. Add some details to your picture that tell more about your favorite movie.

Write about your picture.

Here is a picture of my favorite thing to do:

If it is hard to think of a favorite thing, look at the writing ideas on page 57. If you have *many* favorite things, use one here. Add the rest to the *My Writing Ideas* list on page 57 for later. Don't let any of your good ideas escape!

Write about your picture.

Word Banks

When a carpenter goes to work, she needs a tool box. When someone goes to an office to do work, he might need books, glasses, pens, paper, and maybe a computer or a telephone. These are tools for working. When you write, you need tools, too.

My tools for writing are

_____

_____

_____

_____ .

Another helpful tool for writing is a **word bank**. Word banks hold words that help you get ideas for sentences and help you write about people, places, things, or feelings.

Here is a word bank that may help you write about your favorite animal. The blank lines are for you to add your own words if you wish.

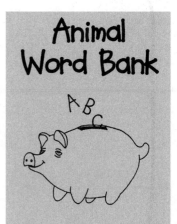

Animal Word Bank

cute

smart

beautiful

fast

funny

clumsy

graceful

soft

playful

cuddly

fuzzy

_____

_____

Here is a picture of my favorite animal:

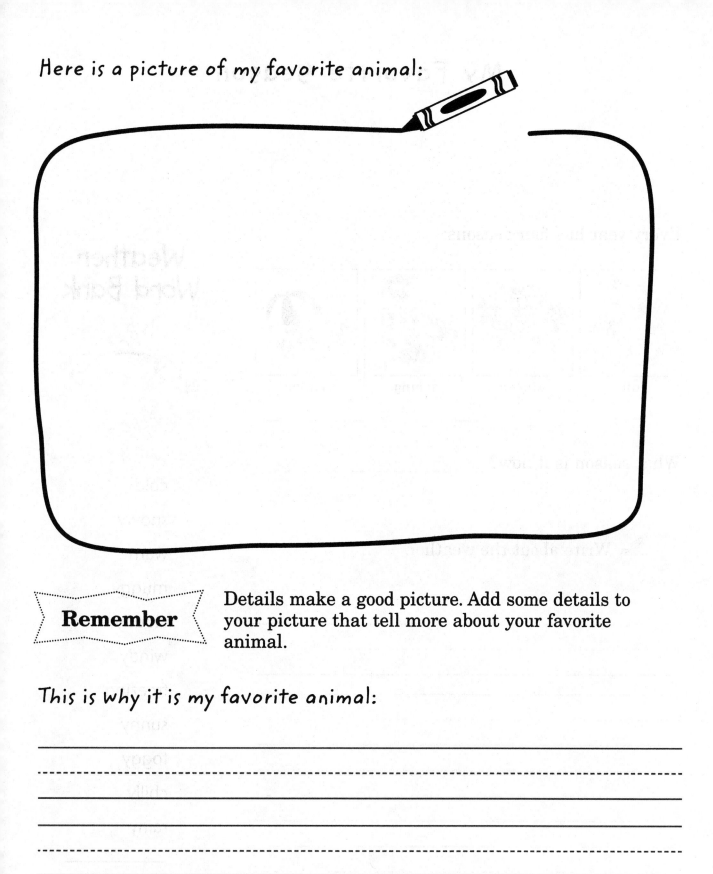

```
┌─────────────────┐
│   Remember   │  Details make a good picture. Add some details to
└─────────────────┘  your picture that tell more about your favorite
                 animal.
```

This is why it is my favorite animal:

_____

- -

_____

- -

_____

- -

_____

My Favorite Season

Every year has four seasons:

fall   winter   spring   summer

_____

What season is it now? _____

✎ Write about the weather.

_____

_____

_____

_____

_____

_____

_____

Weather Word Bank

A B C

cold

snowy

warm

muggy

cloudy

windy

freezing

sunny

foggy

chilly

rainy

_____

_____

Here is a picture of my favorite season:

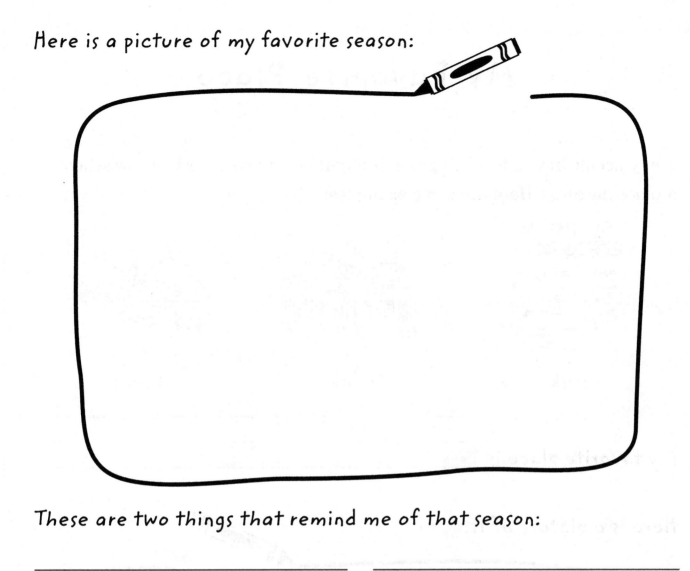

These are two things that remind me of that season:

_____   _____

✎ Write about your picture.

_____

_____

_____

_____

_____

My Favorite Place

Many people have a favorite place. It might be a place near home or school, or a place far away. Here are some examples:

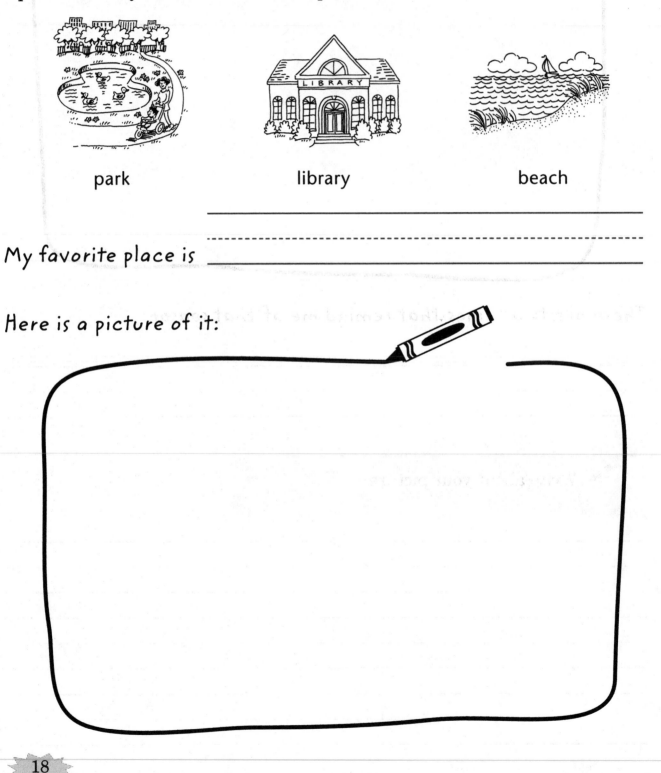

park   library   beach

My favorite place is _____

Here is a picture of it:

✎ Write about your favorite place by answering these questions:

Where is it?

_____

_____

What do you do there?

_____

_____
_____

_____

When do you go there?

_____

_____

Who goes with you?

_____

_____

Why is it your favorite place?

_____

_____

_____

_____

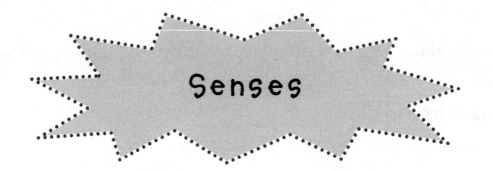

Senses

You use your eyes to see and your ears to hear. You touch with your hands, smell with your nose, and taste with your tongue. When you tell someone what you see, hear, feel, smell, or taste, you use words to describe those sensory things. You might call these words the details. When you add these details to your writing, they make your writing come alive.

seeing

hearing

touching

smelling

tasting

Think about what you see, hear, smell, touch, and taste.

This is something I heard today: _____

It sounded like _____ .

This is something I touched today: _____

It felt _____ .

This is something I tasted today: _____

It tasted _____ .

Read over your writing. If you are stuck on the spelling of a word, do your best and then underline it.

Seeing

Here is a picture of my eyes:

Noticing colors is one way to write about things you see. Here is a word bank filled with color words. Color each box with the right color. Add some of your own words if you wish.

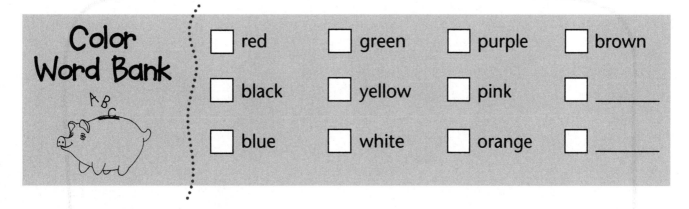

Color Word Bank

☐ red   ☐ green   ☐ purple   ☐ brown

☐ black   ☐ yellow   ☐ pink   ☐ _____

☐ blue   ☐ white   ☐ orange   ☐ _____

Here are some other words to describe things you see. Add some of your own words if you wish.

Seeing Word Bank

big   dull   pretty   tall

small   colorful   long   _____

shiny   bright   short   _____

Here is a picture of something I see at my school:

Use your new word banks to write about your picture.

These are things that I might see in the city or in the country:

City   **Country**

_____   _____

_____   _____

_____   _____

_____   _____

_____   _____

Here are two pictures:

Here is a word bank filled with more describing words.

Describing
Word Bank

crowded	shining	light	open	_____
tall	exciting	green	wooded	_____
busy	majestic	grassy	slow	

✎ Use the word bank above to help you write about your pictures.
Add your own words if you wish.

_____

_____

_____

_____

These are things that I might see on my favorite holiday or celebration:

_____

- -

_____

- -

_____

- -

_____

Here is a picture:

Here are some words to help you write about a holiday or celebration:

Holiday Word Bank

funny	bright	colorful	_____
spooky	happy	scary	_____
sparkly	sunny	glowing	_____

✏️ Use the word bank above to help you write three or four sentences about your picture.

_____

_____

_____

_____

_____

_____

_____

_____

_____

_____

Hearing

I hear with my ears. Here is a picture of my ears:

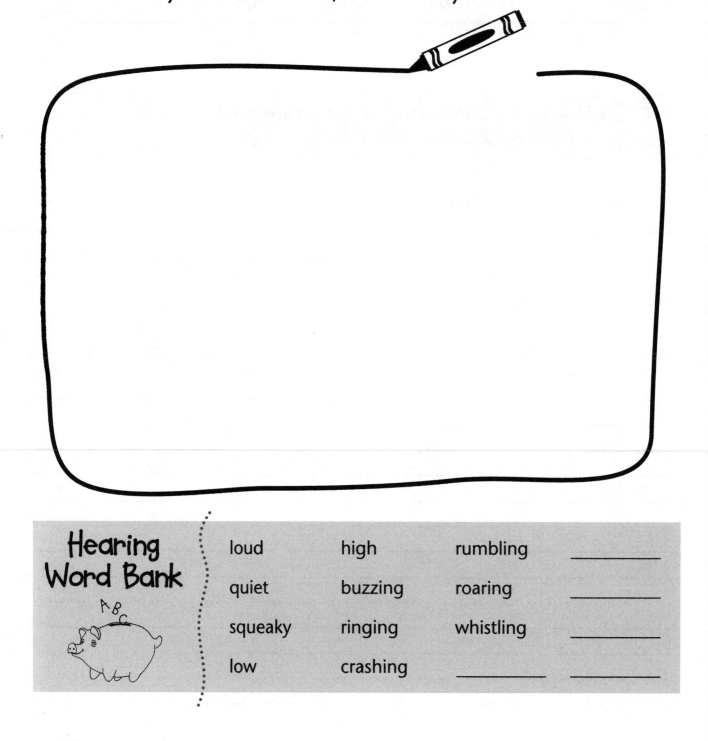

Hearing Word Bank

loud	high	rumbling	_____
quiet	buzzing	roaring	_____
squeaky	ringing	whistling	_____
low	crashing	_____	_____

1. Circle the pictures of the things that make a loud sound.

2. Circle the pictures of the things that make a quiet sound.

3. Circle the picture of the thing that makes a ringing sound.

4. Circle the picture of the thing that makes a buzzing sound.

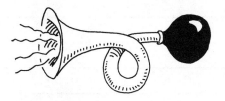 

Here is a picture of a playground:

Here is a list of sounds I might hear on a playground:

Write about your picture.

Here is a picture of a birthday party:

Here is a list of sounds I might hear at a birthday party:

✎ Write about your picture.

31

Here is a picture of the beach:

Here is a list of sounds I might hear at the beach:

Read over your writing. If you are stuck on the spelling of a word, do your best and then underline it.

Smelling

I smell with my nose. Here is a picture of my nose:

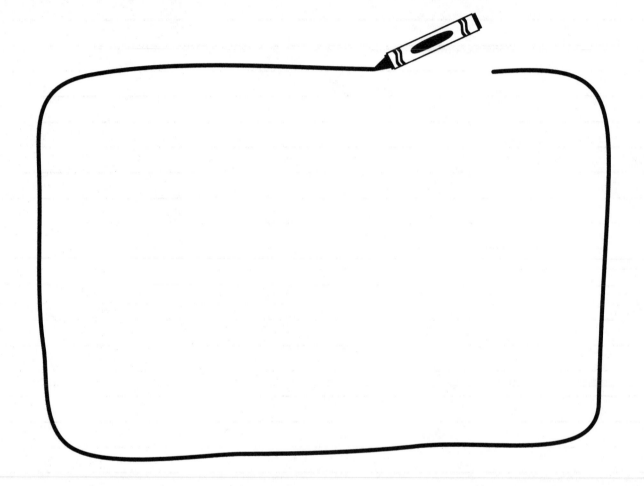

Here are some words you can use to write about how things smell:

Smelling Word Bank			
yummy	fruity	rotten	_____
stinky	fishy	clean	_____
smoky	like flowers	like grass	_____
sweet	burned	_____	_____

(Circle) pictures of the things you like to smell.

ocean

skunk

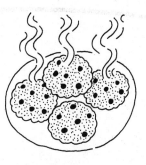

cookies

apple pie

burning toast

flowers

popcorn

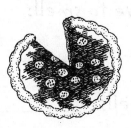

pizza

Here is a picture of something I love to smell:

This is what I love to smell: _____

This is how it smells: _____

I do not like to smell _____

because it smells like _____!

Touching

I feel things when I touch them with my fingers.
Here is a picture of my hand:

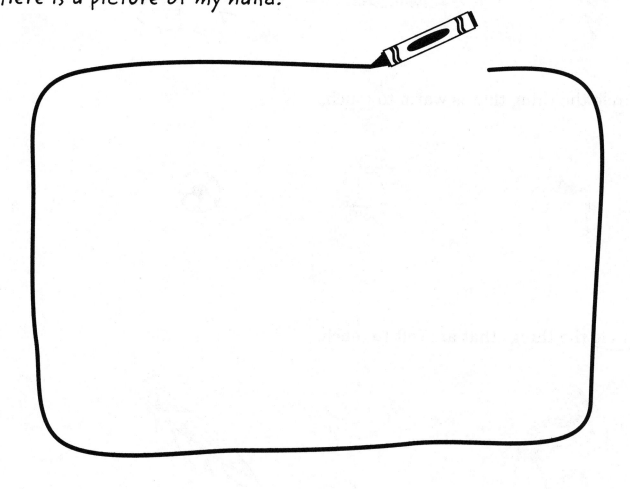

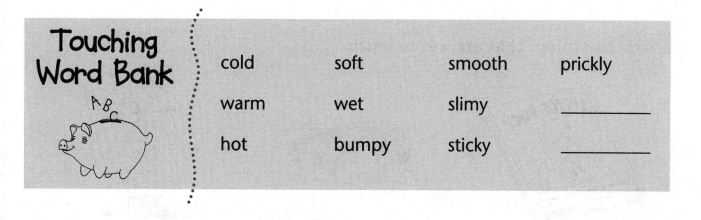

Touching Word Bank

cold	soft	smooth	prickly
warm	wet	slimy	_____
hot	bumpy	sticky	_____

Circle the things that are cold to touch.

Circle the thing that is warm to touch.

Circle the things that are soft to touch.

Circle the things that are wet to touch.

Look around you and pick an object. Draw a picture of it.

✏️ Use some of the words in the **touching** word bank on page 37 to write about how the object feels.

Tasting

Tasting is important. Everyone likes to eat things that taste good, but not everyone likes the same things.

These are some words you could use to write about how something tastes. Add your own words if you wish.

Tasting Word Bank	sweet	dry	bitter	_____
	sour	salty	smooth	_____
	fruity	spicy	crunchy	_____
	creamy	yummy	salty	_____

These are the foods that I think taste good.

_____   _____

_____   _____

_____   _____

_____   _____

_____   _____

Here is a picture of my favorite thing to eat:

I like to eat _____ because it tastes

_____ and _____ .

Pretend you are making a really tall sandwich that includes ALL of your favorite foods. Draw a picture of the sandwich.

The foods in my sandwich are:

_____
- -
_____
_____
- -
_____
_____
_____
_____
- -
_____
_____
- -
_____
_____
- -
_____

_____
- -
My sandwich tastes _____.

All the Senses

Draw a picture of you at home.

List the things you might see, hear, smell, touch, and taste when you are at home.

Draw a picture of you on a picnic.

Can you think of other places you go, or other things you do that use your senses? Add them to the *My Writing Ideas* list on page 57 for later. Don't let any of your good ideas escape!

My Memories

A memory is something you remember that happened in the past. Think about something that happened to you a long time ago or a few days ago. Remember a birthday, a trip, or something about school. Picture it as a movie in your mind.

Draw a picture of your memory.

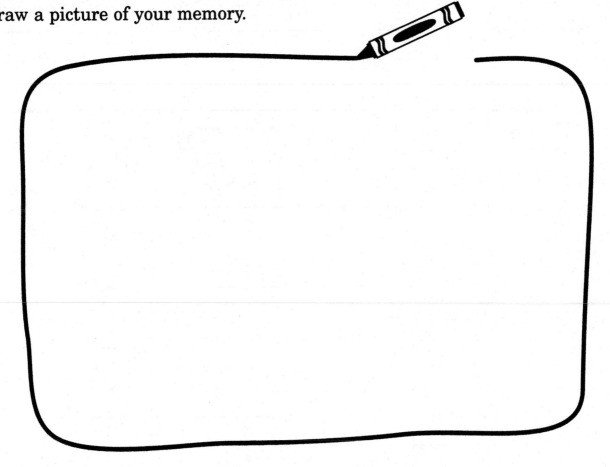

Now, look at your picture. Is there a way to make your picture clearer? Can you use your senses to add some details that would explain your memory better? Add more details to your picture.

Who or *what* does the picture show?

_____

- -

_____

_____

- -

_____

What happened?

_____

- -

_____

_____

- -

_____

Where did it happen?

_____

- -

_____

_____

- -

_____

When did it happen?

_____

- -

_____

_____

- -

_____

Telling a Story

When you write about something that happened, you are telling a story. A story has a **beginning**, a **middle**, and an **end**. You can tell a story about a memory with pictures as on page 49. The first box shows the beginning of the story, the second box shows the middle, and the third box shows the end.

Memories are a good place to start when you want to get ideas for a story. You can use the *My Writing Ideas* list on page 57 to write down memories that you want to write about later.

Draw a picture of the beginning, middle, and end of your story. Then write about each picture on the lines.

Beginning

Middle

End

Now draw another memory in pictures. Show the beginning of the story in the first box, the middle of the story in the second box, and the end of the story in the third box.

First

Then

Finally

Now put the pieces together to write your story!

Read over your writing. If you are stuck on the spelling of a word, do your best and then underline it.

Reread your story on page 51. Add some details: things you might have seen, heard, felt, smelled, or even tasted.

When you want to add something to your story, use a **caret**. A caret looks like this: ∧

Examples

little
The boy ran across the playground.
∧

furry, gray   as fast as
The cat ran home. she could
              ∧   ∧

sweet, pink   yummy
I drank some lemonade with my lunch.
           ∧   ∧

as   as a tree
My brother is tall.
              ∧ ∧

Now see if you can add more detail to these sentences. Don't forget to use a caret!

The car looks funny.   Her garden is over there.

The cat went to sleep.   The boat sailed on the water.

I don't understand. How will a *carrot* help me add details?

It won't! That kind of *carrot* is for eating. This is the *caret* that helps you add details!

On this page, rewrite your story from page 51, this time with more details. If you are unsure about any spellings, just underline the word that you think is misspelled.

Read your story to a friend.

My Imagination

It is fun to use your imagination when you write stories, because you can pretend different things.

Use your imagination to finish these sentences:

If I had magic shoes that would take me anywhere, I would go

_____

_____

_____

_____ .

Here is a picture:

If I met a giant on the way to school, I would say, _____.

Then the giant would say, _____.

Here is a picture:

If I visited the moon, I would see:

Here is a picture:

I would come home from the moon because I would miss

If my friend and I could do anything we wanted, we would

_____

- -

_____

_____

- -

_____

_____

- -

_____

_____

- -

_____

_____

- .

_____

Here is a picture:

Have fun sharing your writing with a friend!

My Writing Ideas

_____   _____
---   ---
_____   _____
---   ---
_____   _____
---   ---
_____   _____
---   ---
_____   _____
---   ---
_____   _____
---   ---
_____   _____
---   ---
_____   _____

More Writing Ideas

my best friend	my biggest wish is that . . .
something that scared me	fun things to do outside
the funniest thing I can remember	I love to pretend . . .
a visit to grandma's house	the best part about school
my favorite meal	a dream
Halloween night	my pet

For the Teacher

beginning	draw	middle	something
buildings	end	movie	special
caret	favorite	neighborhood	squeaky
celebration	fruit	night	straight
change	giant	notice	telephone
circle	happened	people	tools
city	hear	photograph	touch
color	heavier	picture	younger
computer	houses	pieces	warm
correct	imagination	school	weather
country	library	scratchy	would
curly	listen	season	write
describe	many	senses	
details	measured	sentences	
does	memory	some	